All Scripture references taken from the KJV of the Holy Bible, unless otherwise indicated.

WE GET ALONG, *RIGHT? Compatibility Reality for Couples*
by Dr. Marlene Miles
Freshwater Press 2025
freshwaterpress9@gmail.com

ISBN: 978-1-967860-66-1

Paperback Version

Copyright 2025, Dr. Marlene Miles

All rights reserved. No part of this book may be reproduced, distributed, or transmitted by any means or in any means including photocopying, recording or other electronic or mechanical methods without prior written permission of the publisher except in the case of brief publications or critical reviews.

Companion Workbook for this series:

WE GET ALONG, RIGHT?

The Workbook for Couples Who Think *They Do*

Table of Contents

PREFACE 5
INTRODUCTION 7
HOW YA LIVING? 11
OH, THERE'S MORE 14
TIKTOK DOESN'T WARN YOU ABOUT THIS STUFF 19
HOUSEHOLD & LIVING STYLE 24
SLEEP HABITS & BEDTIME CULTURE 29
FOOD, COOKING, & EATING STYLE/Habits 40
MONEY, BILLS & WHY IS AMAZON HERE AGAIN? 52
BATHROOM & HYGIENE REALITIES 60
DRIVING, ERRANDS & TRAVEL and CAR HABITS 67
PHONE, TECH, AND SOCIAL MEDIA BEHAVIOR 77
COMMUNICATION & EMOTIONAL STYLE 84
CLOTHING & PERSONAL ITEMS 92
PETS, KIDS, FAMILY & "OTHER HUMANS YOU DIDN'T MARRY"
.... 95
THE 12 STEPS TO OUT THE DOOR, DUDE: CHEATING 111
The cheating scale no one agrees on — until it's too late. 111
WORK 117
CAN I LIVE WITH THIS? 121
BEFORE YOU CLOSE THIS BOOK 129
Relationship Books by this Author 130
Other books by this author 133
Other Series 138

WE GET ALONG, *RIGHT*?

Compatibility Realities for Couples

PREFACE

Love is beautiful; it is when you see the divine in your partner. Living together is humanity. Living together is when you see the humanity in your spouse. It's the daily grind, paperwork, settings, habits, smells, and thermostat negotiations.

If you're reading this, chances are you're either deeply in love, slightly in love, hopeful about love, or planning out the Pinterest board version of love. Cute. Adorable. Precious.

This book is for you *before* life swings open the door to what I call The Compatibility Trap.

The trap is simple: You think the big things will be the problem. But it's the tiny, daily, stupid things that turn two in-love people into two irritated folks. We want you to remain soulmates and not devolve into roommates, or revolt into jail mates, who secretly Google "Is snoring grounds for annulment?"

Nobody tells you this part. Your friends will hype the proposal. Your mother will ask if "he has a good job." The internet will show you matching pajama sets and wedding hashtags.

What nobody warns you about is this:

- You don't know someone until you've shared a bathroom sink with their toothpaste habits.

- You don't know someone until you've watched them "load" a dishwasher and wonder is that the same way they shove sneakers and athletic gear into a closet.

- You don't know someone until you've survived their idea of "room temperature."

Marriage is not destroyed by *big dramatic moments*. Mostly, it's worn down by 28,000 daily frictions.

` This book is not anti-love; it's pro-reality. It's not here to scare you; it's here to save you. Romantic love is emotional. Compatibility is logistical.

If love is poetry, compatibility is plumbing, sleep patterns, chore distribution, food temperature, and blanket ownership rights.

If you're not married yet, congratulations — you still have choices. If you're not living together yet — even better, because that's where the plot twists start.

This book is the handbook you should've received when dating became "serious," and people started using words like *forever, joint lease, and mortgage.*

Let's begin.

INTRODUCTION

You met, fell in love, or it could have been love at first sight. Well, Hallelujah. But what did you love? Surely it wasn't everything because unless you're bionic or AI or something, you couldn't see everything at first sight. Everyday compatibility flashpoints — the kinds of things that *sound small but turn into World War III if you live together*. Not just the big "values + life goals" list (kids, religion, money), but the *daily grind* issues that either get negotiated, nagged about, or contribute to the slow death of the relationship. They do not show up immediately, they won't--, they can't because everyone is on their best behavior at the beginning, and some, for as long as they can stay on that good behavior.

Oh, we like the same kinds of food. Really? Three years into their relationship after another couple came to dinner and raved about her potato salad, a guy asked a girl, "Why didn't you tell me that your potato salad was so good?"

She was confused and said, "I made potato salad for you many times. The first time, you took the entire bowl, placed it in your lap and ate it all while you watched the football game. That's why I have kept making it for you all these years."

He said, "I just ate that, I didn't know it was good."

She asked, "Then why did you eat it?"

He said, because I was trying to impress you.

Notwithstanding the fakes, you will still never know everything about being with, and especially living with a person instantly. That's why living your everyday life with a person can be challenging, or nearly impossible.

Rita looked across the lake from the luxury condo she lived in, she pointed and said, "My husband, Greg lives over there."

I said, "Over where?"

She said, "In those condos over there." Then she continued, "I love him and he loves me, but we just can't live together. If I come in the house and it's hot, then I will turn on the air and I don't want to hear anything he has to say about that. If I come in the house and it's cold, then I will turn on the heat. His opinion about those things are not worth fighting over, so we live in two separate houses."

"Rita!"

"Yes, it's true. We've been married 50 years now, I'm 72 she said. Then she laughed and said, he's says he's going to get a row boat to come and see me."

You don't really know someone until you share a thermostat, a bathroom, or a blanket, that is why "compatibility" is not romantic but essential.

She--, *who is **she***? She could be anyone dating anyone. So, *she* thought she was marrying a man. Turns out she was marrying a person who believes 'airing the house out' is the same as turning on the AC."

"Dear Reader after all she found out, after all any of us find out, do we still marry him? Love is powerful. So is denial." If you think you can fix this after the wedding, rethink it. Not married yet. Mostly early-daters, young adults, or "we're in love and nothing could ever go wrong" believers--, people who still think compatibility is about *vibes* and not *thermostats, snoring, and toothbrush caps--, this book is for you.*

If you're still in the stage where you think 'we never argue, we're soulmates, just wait until you see how they grocery shop. Wait until you find out that neither of you know how to make coffee.

This book may be the reality check nobody else gives you—not to depress you, but to prepare you. There will be a lot of things brought up in this book, and you are now charged to ask yourself about any of those things: "Can I live with this for the next 40 years without developing a stress twitch?"

Yes, love is about how your partner treats you. But when you see how they treat the trash, the bathroom, the laundry basket and the coat closet, you may think differently about them than you do right now. I'm writing this, I'm telling you this so you can brace yourself. Yes, brace yourself and keep on loving each other. I intend to take the shock out of anything that could shock you once the two of you are married.

Small things that you think don't matter, but will 100% matter is what the book is about. Like when their mother comes over and rearranges your kitchen because you didn't do it right. Or when their sister comes over and reports back to their mother and they come to rescue their child from your "way of living."

HOW YA LIVING?

Where "I love you" meets "why is every cabinet door open?"

Room Temperature Control

- One wants the AC at 65° year-round in warmer climates and 9 months out of the year in zones that have seasons, either because that is a comfortable temperature for them, or it is because they are saving money.

Watch out, if you divide up bills in the house—especially if you divide up utility payments. Your partner may want to save on the utilities that they are responsible for and freely use the utilities whose bills you are responsible to pay. That is more than a issue of comfort or discomfort, it is an issue of selfishness and honesty.

Sarah pays the water bill at she and Bob's suburban home, so in the summer, during grass growing season, Bob doesn't mind turning on the sprinkler system every day, sometimes twice a day. Bob pays the electric bill, so the AC is set at 83 degrees Fahrenheit. This is more than a compatibility issue, but it must be addressed honestly and dealt with. Sarah pays the gas bill, so it's fine with

Bob if the inside temperature of the home is 83 degrees in the wintertime and if the gas fireplace is on every night, even all night, overnight.

- One thinks 83° is a normal temperature in the hot months "because it saves money." Well, in the summer, but that same person would be content with 65 degrees in the winter, because that would also save money. To them, it's not about comfort, safety or even health--, it's about money.

Windows Open vs Closed

- One loves fresh air. The other thinks outside air is "dirt entering the home."
- One wants the AC off because it is cooler outside than in the house. (And how will that air get in here? The other will ask.)

Household Scents

- One loves essential oils and candles.
- The other gets a headache from anything scented.

(Warning: This could be a medical issue; fragrances can trigger anything from allergic reactions to migraines to full blown asthma attacks.)

Noise Tolerance

- One needs peace and quiet, in either order.
- The other is a "phone-on-speaker, TV-on-100, music-in-every-room" person, constantly.

Clutter vs Clean Freak

- One calls it "organized chaos."
- The other calls it "a crime scene."

These are real, and real life problems and issues. These are the things that you learn about a person when you two are getting to know each other. It is part of why you get to know one another. Here is a secret: Once you have sex with a person (or start having sex with them) they stop trying to get to know you. And that is a fact. So, it would be better to find out all of this stuff or as much as you can before you have sex with them. Ideally, sex is supposed to wait until marriage. We all should know this, though: spending time with another will transfer some of their traits and behaviors to you. Having sex with another will transfer MANY of their traits and behaviors to you, even if you break up with them later, or end up not liking them, you will still be "like" them--, even the traits you don't like about them.

Females pick up A LOT from males.

OH, THERE'S MORE

Tasha knew she was in trouble the day she walked into the kitchen and saw Mark lovingly rinsing out the same sponge they'd been using since as long as she could remember. "Mark, throw that thing out," she said.

"It's still good," he said, squeezing grayish-brown dishwater from its spongy corpse. That was the day she learned love is blind, but bacteria are not.

Dishcloth vs Sponge

- One uses a fresh dishcloth daily.
- The other keeps one bacteria-soaked sponge for 8 months. And will argue that the sponge is more sanitary than the dishcloth.

Hygiene

- Handwashing in general. One may obsessively wash like OCD, Mr. Monk, and the other thinks, I took a shower this morning, there was lots of soap in the shower. My hands are still clean from my morning shower, even though it's now dinner time.

- Kitchen hygiene: Eating off spoons and putting them back into dishes.
- Double dipping.
- Applying the 5 second rule when the bacon falls on the floor. (Cooked or even before it is cooked.)
- One man thinks it is okay to wipe his mouth with the dishtowel, as if it is a giant dinner napkin. The other is appalled, having never seen such as that before.

Washing Dishes

- Immediately after eating" vs Soak it for three days until it becomes a science experiment.

Handling a Mess

- Cleans it while it happens vs walks past it 12 times until asked.

Leaving the Cap Off Things

- Toothpaste, milk, orange juice —is chaos. Can she leave the cap off something in his garage? Can he leave the cap off her nail polish?

Grocery Store Behavior

- Focused mission vs wanders, adds 12 snacks, forgets detergent.

Is a Green-Fiend: Saves Gift Bags and Tissue Paper

- Reuse forever vs throws everything away immediately.
- Recycles religiously vs "what's the point, it all goes to the same place."

Recycling Reality

- One believes in saving the planet.
- One believes recycling is "a scam invented by Big Plastic."

Sharing Food

- One is "sure, have a bite." Would share down to the last spaghetti noodle, like the lady and the tramp.
- The other guards their plates like a prison tray.

Fridge Organization

- Labels, sections, and zones… vs… "put it anywhere there's space."
- Uncovered things in the fridge. Really? That's gross.
- There is ½ an inch of orange juice or milk in the container because one doesn't want to throw the milk carton away.
- Drinking out of the juice jar or the milk carton.

Trash Overflow Tolerance

- One takes it out when it's ¾ full.
- One takes it out when it is ½ full, in the middle of dinner prep.
- The other who is preparing the meal doesn't see the trash gone looks in the trash bin and there is no liner in it all of a sudden.
- The other waits until it's Jenga-stacked and falling out.

Trash Levels You Can Live With

- One takes it out when it's ¾ full.
- One waits until it's overflowing like a volcano of poor decisions.

Trash vs Garbage – does your person know the difference? Do they know what a garbage disposer is and how ot use it? What goes in it and what does not?

Trashcan Hygiene – one rinses foodstuff off of containers or opened cans vs the other who just throws containers or cans of food into the trashcan all smelly and gross.

Food Container Hoarder vs Throw-It-Away-*er*

- "These old takeout containers are reusable!" "No, this is how hoarding shows up one lid at a time."

To-Go Cup Hoarder

- Saves 57 empty Starbucks cups "just in case."

These are just a few things that couples may have conflict about. In this book we will categorize them, share a story and at the end of each section list them again for discussion or study.

REVIEW BOX:

Dishcloth vs Sponge

Hygiene

Washing Dishes:

Handling a Mess

Leaving the Cap Off Things

Grocery Store Behavior

Is a Green-Fiend: Saves Gift Bags and Tissue Paper

Recycling Reality

Sharing Food

Fridge Organization

Trash Overflow Tolerance

Trash Levels You Can Live With

Trash vs Garbage

Food Container Hoarder vs Throw-It-Away-*er*

To-Go Cup Hoarder

TIKTOK DOESN'T WARN YOU ABOUT THIS STUFF

Store Returns

- Takes a return back the same week vs keeps it in the trunk for 8 months.
- Worse, takes **everything** back about a week after purchased. Stores won't accept their returns anymore because they return everything sooner or later.

Household Noise in the Morning

- Ninja quiet vs slams every cabinet like it owes them money.
- Inconsiderate: If I'm up, everyone must be up.

Talking During Sports / TV

- One watches in silence.
- One wants to scream and yell at the TV and the referees.
- One yells at the characters in the movie.
- The other wants to discuss *feelings* during the 4th quarter.

- One has no idea what has happened during the movie because they were asleep through most of it.

Replacing the Toilet Paper

- Instantly.
- Or they just leave the cardboard tube like a memorial, as if that can be magically, urgently softened and used as bathroom paper.

Shoes on in the House

- Mandatory removal vs "my feet are already in motion."

Refrigerator Door Closing

- **Fully sealed click vs "closed enough."**

Home Décor Battles

- Minimalist white walls vs "more throw pillows, more art, more everything."
- One wears sunglasses in the house because beige is too bright for the wall that used to be generic white.
- It's obvious that one of you can't decorate, but neither of you think it's you...

Snacks in Bed

- Forbidden vs crumbs are part of life.

Power Nap Philosophy

- 20 mins max vs "I'll lay down at 3 and wake up tomorrow."

How They Treat Servicepeople

- Respectful vs low-key rude.

Immediate vs Delayed Replies

- Texts back fast vs vanishes for 7 hours.

Excitement Level for Other People's Babies

- "Aww, so cute!" vs "Why is it staring at me?"
- Stop cooing over those babies; people don't like it when you speak to their child. *What*?

Sleeping With the TV On

- Needs total silence vs needs background noise to sleep.

How They Open Packages

- Uses scissors, keeps box tidy vs rips it open like a raccoon.
- Puts things back where they belong, versus everything is just laying wherever it was used like letter openers and boxcutters. .

Voice Volume at Home

- Indoor voice vs full stadium projection.

Closing Cabinet Doors

- Closes them vs leaves them open like ghost portals.

Do They Actually Read Instructions

- Reads manual vs builds furniture by instinct and rage.

Can't build or fix anything but is willing to pay the handyman who can vs. the other who just leaves unassembled or broken things in the middle of the floor for a year.

Maybe none of this bothers you. Well good. But if it does if compatibility cannot be reached, the peace of the house will fall on one and possibly not the other. Eventually, that could lead to resentment. So, if little living idiosyncrasies bother you, get to know your person before you make them your spouse. Couples can fight over the stupidest things. If a little water on the bathroom floor, or a hair in the bathroom sink freaks you out, this needs to be discussed sooner than later.

Not to be funny, but some behaviors might be because your partner is simply lazy and disorganized. It could be that they don't have any home training. But be sure they are not unhappy or depressed. Depressed people may be functional in the work environment, but at home, these behaviors as the ones discussed so far may show up.

Now we will add more potential flashpoints of living together, group organized for better use and discussion. I hope you will discuss this book with someone—or others.

REVIEW BOX:

Store Returns

Household Noise in the Morning

Talking During Sports / TV

Replacing the Toilet Paper

Shoes in the House

Refrigerator Door Closing

Home Décor Battles

Snacks in Bed

Power Nap Philosophy

How They Treat Servicepeople

Excitement Level for Other People's Babies

Sleeping With the TV On

How They Open Packages

Voice Volume at Home

Closing Cabinet Doors'

Do They Actually Read Instructions

Can't build or fix anything

HOUSEHOLD & LIVING STYLE

When Brisa and Jordan first started dating, everything was perfect. They laughed at the same memes, ordered the same Starbucks drink, and said things like "we're so in sync, it's crazy."

Then she went to his apartment for the first full weekend.

On day one, she discovered:

- He never closes kitchen drawers or cabinet doors.
- His dishes "soak" for 72 hours.
- The silverware that is actually in a drawer is thrown in, not organized in the slots of the utensil holder.
- His trash can was full —well, when he didn't miss the trashcan completely, and had been full — since the Obama era.

By Sunday, she wasn't wondering if he loved her. She was wondering if she could legally burn a sponge in his sink as an act of self-defense. That's when she realized: Compatibility isn't romance. It's lifestyle habits you have to live with every day.

REAL-LIFE COMPATIBILITY TRAPS

Dishcloth vs Sponge Philosophy

- A sponge should be replaced weekly vs This sponge has emotional value.

Some people clean. Others *just move bacteria around with confidence.* You cannot use a sponge you clean the bathroom with to do the dishes, to wash the car. Sponges shouldn't travel like that.

Dishes: Wash Now vs Let Them Become Fossils

- One rinses immediately.
- The other says "I'll get to it" until it becomes an archeological layer.
- One knows the way from the dining table to the kitchen sink; the other doesn't and just leaves their plate on the table.

Dishwashing Rules

- One rinses everything before loading and insists that is how it must be done.
- The other throws a plate in with half a pancake still stuck to it.

Lights Off vs Lights Everywhere

- "Turn off the lights when you leave a room."
- "I like ambiance. All the time. Always."

Some people live in a house. Others live in a lighthouse.

- One turns lights off religiously.

- The other treats the house like Times Square.

Organized Chaos" vs "Everything Has a Label"

- One uses bins, systems, and color coding.
- The other says, "I know exactly where everything is," and it's a *lie*.

Fridge Logic

- Organized shelves by category
- Or "I will put the milk wherever it can fit in.

BEFORE YOU GET MARRIED, ASK YOURSELF:

Can I live with this—for 50 years—without planning an escape route or writing a true-crime monologue in my head?

☐ Yes
☐ No
☐ I need to lie down and think

    A fellow picked me up for a date. When I got into his vehicle there were four or five empty bottles or cups on the floor where my feet should go. He reached down and picked up his Stanley cup, I suppose, so my feet wouldn't hurt it and left all that other trash beneath my feet. I could not believe it. I should have gotten out of the vehicle right then, but he was already driving when he did that. I did not return to the scene of that car after that day.

What could compromise look like?

Am I being petty... or is this actually who they are every single day?

REVIEW BOX:

Store Returns

Household Noise in the Morning

Talking During Sports / TV

Replacing the Toilet Paper

Shoes in the House

Dryer Lint Trap

Folding vs Stuffing Laundry

Refrigerator Door Closing

Home Décor Battles

Snacks in Bed

Power Nap Philosophy

How They Treat the Waitstaff

Immediate vs Delayed Replies

Excitement Level for Other People's Babies

Sleeping With the TV On

How They Open Packages

Voice Volume at Home

Closing Cabinet Doors'

Do They Actually Read Instructions

Can't build or fix anything

SLEEP HABITS & BEDTIME CULTURE

Marriage begins when the snoring starts.

Speaking of sleep habits, it's all fun and romantic until you realize the love of your life sleeps like a rotisserie chicken and their snoring sounds like a diesel engine in a thunderstorm.

You can survive bad communication, but can you really survive 7 years of being slapped in the face at 2am by a human windmill.

Speaking of sleeping, is it okay for the pets to be in the bed? How about the kids? Better talk about it now instead of when it happens because with pets and kids if it happens once, it is either heartbreaking to stop it or it is impossible to stop because you don't want to break their hearts.

Whether the Bed Must Be Made Daily

- "Make it every morning" vs "Why, I'm getting back in it tonight." Not to encourage laziness, but some studies say that you should let the bed air out a bit before making it in the morning because of the moisture from sweating and what not is still in the sheets and possibly on the mattress. They say it's more sanitary. But, hey—do your own research.

Personal Space

- One wants cuddles 24/7.
- The other wants "my side of the couch, and my side of the bed. PLEASE." *Why are you touching me?*

Thermostat at Night vs Day (that again?) YUP!

- Freezing to sleep, warm during day vs opposite cycle.

Maria couldn't sleep for years with her husband. She kept waking up at night feeling like something was crawling on her. **It was sweat.** The thermostat was set at 83 degrees Fahrenheit, all year.

Eating in Bed

- Absolutely not vs "popcorn crumbs are part of the movie experience."

TV in the bedroom or not argument.

Snoring

- Enough said.

Two college students get married young, discover they literally sleep like two different species. One is "lights off, white noise, blackout curtains" — the other scrolls TikTok at full brightness in bed.

- One needs total darkness + silence.
- The other falls asleep to TV blasting or scrolling TikTok and forgets not to laugh out loud at the funniest videos. This one needs the noise in order to sleep, if it is too dark or too quiet, they can't rest.

Romance is cute. Sleep is survival.

First sleepover goes great... until there's snoring like a freight train. Remember, once you sleep with him, he's done getting to know you. Do you now know enough about him? Because that works both ways.

One person sleeps like a corpse, the other like they're fighting invisible ninjas

Dog (or cat) jumps in bed like it pays rent

Blue-light phone face at 1am

One needs silence, one needs "fan + rain + ocean + spaceship noise"

Mattress Firmness

One wants the firmness of the mattress a little harder than the floor, the other wants cloud softness, no support. Of course, Sleep Number may solve that if that is within your budget. We had a Sleep Number bed and my husband couldn't even find a number that worked for him; he changed it every night and complained about the mattress every morning. We gave it away.

Blanket theft incident- invasion of the covers snatcher. There is a covers hog on the loose. **Cover Hog** vs Cold Toe Survivor. Why are you putting your cold feet on me?! Even your butt is cold, push over! Vs. the cuddler who wants their spouse to warm them up as they fall asleep.

Multiple snooze settings: Alarm clock is set for 5:45 am, and 5:47 am, 5:49 am, 5:51 am—and it is across the room, so somebody has got to get up to turn it off. (You all need Alexa.)

REFLECTION BOX:

"Could I do this for the next 50 years?" _____

"Who wins the blanket by default?"

_____

"Would this be cute at date #5… but a felony at year #5?"

_____

When Alexis and Trey first got married sleeping together was magical. They'd fall asleep in each other's arms, wrapped up in romance, hormones, and denial.

Then came the first full week together.

Night 1:
She discovers he snores like someone is slowly choking a walrus. He claims, "I don't snore, you just heard me breathing with passion."

Night 2:

He grinds his teeth like a freight train. She elbows him. He complains, falls back to sleep right away and starts grinding his teeth again – between snores.

Night 2:
He wakes up freezing because she stole the entire blanket and cocooned herself like a burrito with trust issues.

Night 3:
She tries to go to sleep at 10pm. He decides that's the perfect time to eat chips in bed while watching YouTube conspiracy videos… on full brightness.

Night 4:
His dog — a 65-pound "baby" — jumps onto the bed at 3am, lands directly on her stomach, and sighs like *she* is the one invading *his* space.

Night 5:
She sets one gentle alarm and wakes up.
He sets nine alarms — 6:00, 6:05, 6:07, 6:10, 6:11, 6:13 — and sleeps through all of them like he's auditioning for a coma study.

By Night 7, Alexis realized:
No one warns you about sleep compatibility. Is it because they want you to learn the hard way? Oof!

But I'm your friend, that's why I'm telling you.

If Kyle goes to sleep before Kayla, she won't be able to fall asleep because of Kyle's snoring.

Kyle does not believe that he snores. But he does. So Kayla recorded him one night after all, she was awake.

If Kayla goes to sleep before Kyle she won't be able to sleep if Kyle stops snoring because then it's too quiet. So she recorded him again to let him know that he has sleep apnea. So, if he is not snoring she can't sleep either because she is worried about him.

Kyle will not go for a sleep study because he grew up heavy, lost a lot of weight and has maintained slimness for 20 years and believes that sleep studies are for heavy people. He does not want to be classified as heavy ever again because he was teased so much as a child.

Kayla is exhausted.

WHY THIS MATTERS

Anybody can be in love at 2 p.m., but compatibility is measured at 2 a.m.

Sleep is not *just* sleep — it reveals:

- Comfort habits
- Control issues
- Respect levels
- Self-awareness
- Ability to compromise
- Ability to function the next day at work.

- And whether someone is capable of *turning off a phone like a civilized mammal*

If you can't rest in peace (while still alive) next to them, don't marry them.

REAL COMPATIBILITY TRAPS: SLEEP EDITION

The Snorer vs Sleeping Beauty

- One dreams peacefully.
- The other dreams of pressing a pillow over their face.

Snoring is not "adorable" when it's 4 hours long and your soul is vibrating.

The Blanket Thief vs **The Freezer Survivor**

- One wraps themselves like a cinnamon roll.
- The other wakes up clinging to the edge of a bedsheet… and life.

If you marry a blanket thief, invest in your own comforter now. Save your sanity later.

The Human Furnace vs The Polar Bear

- Some people emit heat like a dragon.
- Others crawl into the bed like "is there a glacier I can borrow?"
- You're not just marrying a person. You're marrying their body temperature.

Pets in the Bed

- "No animals in the bed."
- "My cat sleeps on my chest and purrs into my soul."
- The pet always wins. You are the outsider.

Night Owl vs Early Bird

- 10pm: one says "let's sleep."
- 10pm: the other says "let's reorganize the closet and start a documentary."
- You're not just planning a life together — you're planning *timelines of consciousness*.

Total Silence vs Noise Machine / TV / TikTok

- One needs darkness and dead quiet.
- The other falls asleep to Netflix, ocean waves, or a YouTuber explaining ancient aliens—or all of the preceding.
- If you can hear it, you can't un-hear it.

Phone Glow at 1AM

- Some people scroll with dim light and headphones.
- Others hold a phone 2 inches from their face like they're trying to tan their retinas.
- If your partner's face is lit like a haunted campfire story, this is your sign.

One Pillow vs Pillow Kingdom

- One person: "I need one pillow."

- Other person: "I need 11 pillows, 2 body pillows, and a knee wedge or I can't function."
- Your bed is either a cloud or a battlefield of fluff.

Alarm Clock Compatibility.

- One sets one alarm, wakes up, and moves on with dignity.
- The other sets 14 alarms, starting at 5am, and sleeps through all of them until you question love, life, and the legalities of homicide.
- If you're the wake-first person, you're already TIRED.

Sleep Fighter vs **Peaceful Sleeper** (everybody wasn't Kung Fu fighting).

- One sleeps still like a calm angel.
- The other kicks, rolls, elbows, and occasionally roundhouse-kicks the air.
- If someone sleeps like they're fighting ghosts… you *will* get hit.

BEFORE YOU GET MARRIED, ASK YOURSELF:

Could I live with this, every night, for the next 50 years… and NOT become a true crime documentary?

☐ Yes
☐ No
☐ I need to think about this very, very seriously

Whose sleep habits are the problem — theirs, mine, or BOTH?

_____

_____

Solution ideas before marriage, not after: Separate blankets, sleep mask, earplugs, therapy, sleep deliverance. Sleeping poorly is an affliction, and it can be healed. Any or all of these things may not be happening day one of the marriage but may evolve over time as people grow and age together.

REVIEW BOX:

Personal Space

Thermostat at Night vs Day (that again?) YUP!

Eating in Bed

TV in the bedroom or not argument.

Snoring

One person sleeps like a corpse

Dog (or cat) jumps in bed

Blue-light phone face at 1am

One needs silence

Mattress Firmness

Blanket theft incident-

Multiple snooze settings

The Snorer

The Blanket Thief

The Human Furnace

Pets in the Bed

Night Owl vs Early Bird

Total Silence vs Noise Machine

Phone Glow at 1AM

One Pillow

Alarm Clock Compatibility

Sleep Fighter vs Peaceful Sleeper

FOOD, COOKING, & EATING STYLE/Habits

Love is romantic. Eating together is anthropology.

When Destiny and Malik first started dating, food was part of the romance. She'd cook, he'd show up with compliments and an appetite, and life was sweet—because she was the one seasoning everything.

Then one day, Malik announced, "I'll cook tonight."

Destiny was excited. She sat at the table, waiting. Then she heard it: No chopping, no sizzling, no spice jars rattling. Just… silence. Too much silence. She walked into the kitchen and found Malik calmly sprinkling exactly three grains of salt over raw chicken like he was blessing it before burial.

"Babe, don't you use seasoning?" she asked politely.

Malik smiled, confident and relaxed, saying "I don't measure," he said. "I cook with my spirit. Plus, too much salt is not good for you." His spirit, it turned out, was deeply unseasoned. The chicken tasted like hospital food in witness protection.

That was the night Destiny learned that a man can be sweet, but have no sense of taste, whatsoever.

Will it be daily nourishment or daily arguments? Some people have very sensitive stomachs, others have sensitive tastebuds; some have both. You're a foodie but your spouse has no taste buds—either burned out by spices, or never developed. Lunchables in the 5th grade is the level where they stopped developing tastebuds, and their spice level.

- *Can you love someone who eats gas station sushi and drinks from the carton?*

Food Preferences

- One eats organic, gluten-free, and only eats alkaline water. That's their lifestyle, and you can tell it.
- The other lives on Hot Cheetos, Red Bull, and gas-station nachos--, and you can smell it.

Meal Planning

One makes a religion of creating a weekly grocery list vs ordering DoorDash 6 nights a week.

Leftovers

- Eats everything until it's gone vs lets it rot until the Tupperware gives up.
- I can't eat leftovers, says the other. Period.

- You are either team "save it" or team "why is this still here?"
- To one, leftovers aren't even good enough for the family dog.
- "Leftovers are life; the flavors don't even meld until the next day."
- "If it's been in the fridge more than 6 minutes, throw it out."

Household Chores

- One thinks chores should be split equally.
- The other thinks "I mow the lawn once a month, so we're even."

Loading the Dishwasher

- Plates by size, cutlery sorted… vs… "just shove it in and hope."
- Safety first. The other has turned the utensils into weapons because they are all loaded dangerously.
- Rinse first, or just throw things in the machine?

Grocery Shopping

- In, out, with a list vs "wanders, touches everything, forgets the milk."
- Name brand loyalty or store brand shamelessness?

Paper Towels Usage

- "One sheet is enough" vs "I use half a roll to wipe a drip."

When Is It 'Clean'?

"Sanitized" vs "visible debris cleared." "Kitchen neat freak vs kitchen hurricane"

What happens when dating-era *"aww cute"* turns into "why do you eat like that"? While dating, they were amazed saying, Wow! "We like all the same foods!" — until they actually live together and discover they do NOT. One or both of them was acting.

She cooks… he "seasons" things off of TikTok not knowing that *'Everybody Is So Creative'* is a parody channel.

He eats everything burning-hot in temperature; he microwaves his coffee as soon as he pours it from the coffee machine because it's not hot enough.

Not, Not, Not: She eats everything room temp and re-microwaves nothing. She hates the microwave—even for popcorn.

The hottest coffee? Yes, and the same with food: "Hot food vs room-temp food eater."

Kitchen Drama - They eat out fine, but once they share a fridge… chaos erupts.

Cooking - To one, cooking is the same as high school science lab—everything must be exact. The other lives by, I don't measure, I freestyle'"

Food Doneness - How do you like your food cooked? Raw, half cooked, well done?

Eating at the table vs eating on the couch vs eating *in bed when it's not even breakfast in bed on Mother's Day."*

Using plates vs eating straight from pan/pot"

"Different spice tolerance (Pepper is spicy vs ghost pepper is almost hot enough."

"Fridge is labeled and logical vs fridge is a random cold jungle" full of mysteries.

Cleaning as you cook vs tornado kitchen aftermath

Microwave reheater vs stove reheater

Saving vs Throwing Away plastic Containers

- "These are perfectly good reusable storage!" vs "This is a hoarding problem."
- The other saves every kind of container, the butter tub, the feta cheese tub, and everything else.

There is at least one who won't throw away anything. There could be a dozen empty water bottles lined up on the kitchen counter. Why? Recycling? No, they think the bottles are "still good."

- Aluminum foil is rinsed and is on the dish drying rack.
- Alongside rinsed out zip lock bags. (You tell me.)

Cooking Frequency

- Loves to cook vs sees the kitchen as hostile territory.
- Comes into the kitchen to help, but eats all the bacon as soon as it is cooked so there is none for the meal.

Table Eater vs Couch Eater vs Bed Eater vs just walking around with the food in their hand.

- "Meals happen at a table like grown adults."
- "I eat on the couch watching shows."
- "I will absolutely eat spaghetti in bed and live my truth."
- I don't have time to seat, gotta eat and run.

These are three different species of people.

Spice Tolerance

- One cries eating mild salsa.
- The other carries hot sauce in their bag like a legal weapon.
- Then he says to her, "*This*—what you've made would be good if it had any flavor." He meant heat.

Yes, there is a temperature where love melts.

Refrigerator Logic

- Organized by shelf, labels, categories.

- Random chaos like "Why are the apples next to the raw chicken?"
- Everything goes in the same place, always vs Just throw it in there.
- A fridge is a personality test. Take notes.

WHY THIS MATTERS

You're not just sharing love; nourishment is important and satisfaction with meals is a must. You're not marrying their personality. You're marrying: their food safety beliefs (or lack thereof). their leftover logic – are they a waster or a saver? Do they have secret stomach issues. (maybe you can help them with this.)

- their approach to seasoning, reheating, and dishes
- and how they behave when "hangry"
- Humans can bond over food—or resent each other over it.

Frank complained every time Marla got a small carton of her favorite ice cream. Every bite, he had something to say about her choice to even have a sweet dessert. Didn't she think she was gaining weight, he'd taunt, even while he was eating his favorite ice cream. She did not enjoy herself at all. So, now Marla stops at the store gets her favorite, comes home early from work, eats her ice cream in peace before Frank gets home. This is a bad habit for both of them. If Frank wants to eat half of the sweet potato pie, then he does, Marla has never given him a moment of grief about it. Grace is a gift, and it is a power, especially in a marriage.

And this you should have learned in grade school, do not bad talk what someone is trying to enjoy saying, "Oh gross, how can you stand cottage cheese? It is so nasty, and it smells bad---." Shut up and let the person enjoy what they enjoy and you keep on eating those pork skins that you love so much. Grace is a gift, and it is a power—get some, give some.

Nothing destroys romance faster than watching someone eat yogurt with a fork *just because it was the first utensil they saw.* In defense of the yogurt eaters who use forks, I was one of those people because I hated yogurt and I was trying to train myself to like it. I had a cup of yogurt, and I ate a fork-*not-full* each day, actually for a month. I still don't like it, but I eat it because it is good for me. If your partner's choice of utensils to eat with bothers you--, maybe it's you and not them.

Some people should stay out of the kitchen if they know nothing about food safety. Bernice, aged 29 and a half, just found out that opened mayonnaise goes in the refrigerator, not the pantry. People with no food safety understanding or skills should stay out of the kitchen, so they don't hurt or kill anyone.

There are some who put everything in the refrigerator. I can really be your friend now when I tell you that one night I opened a chip bag but couldn't find a clip and I was so tired that night I didn't feel like looking, so I put the chips in the refrigerator. Folks, let me tell you; there is no humidity in the fridge, so my chips, popcorn and everything stays crunchy in the fridge for weeks and weeks.

You are welcome.

Madge loves to entertain. Her table is amazing for every dinner party. Madge can't cook. Why no one has told her all these years, I don't know. Her husband pushes the food around on the plate and then sneaks to the kitchen later for nourishment. He's really been hungry since he retired because before he did have a hearty lunch each day. He's thin; she's thin. She cooks as though they haven't paid their gas bill; everything is pretty much raw because she is so careful not to burn anything or "dry it out." Woman! Please at least dry out the blood in the chicken.

Graciously, he takes his wife out to eat often, and she loves it, not knowing it's because of her lack of cooking skills. *Bless his heart.*

REAL COMPATIBILITY TRAPS: FOOD EDITION

Seasoning Level One seasons like a Southern grandmother. The other thinks black pepper is "too spicy."

Stone was disgusted and got up from the table to throw his plate of food out. His wife, Tessa stopped him just in time, asking him, Why are you throwing your dinner away?

He said, "Because there's a fruit fly or some small black insect in it." Tessa took a good look and let him know, "Stone, that's *pepper*."

Love is blind, but your tastebuds are fully awake.

Cooking Style: Chef vs Chaos

- One cooks, cleans, and plates like a restaurant. The other uses every pot, pan, and plate… then walks away like the kitchen will heal itself overnight.

Meal Plan vs Wing It

- One says, "Let's grocery shop for the week."
- The other says, "Why are you always planning? Let's just see what happens." But the last time we didn't plan we had Chinese food for Thanksgiving because nothing else was open and we had nothing from the grocery store.
- Spoiler: what happens is $82 worth of takeout and regret.

BEFORE YOU GET MARRIED, ASK:

Could I eat like this for decades without turning into a food villain?

☐ Yes
☐ No
☐ Not unless I start a secret seasoning savings account

Does this person respect food... or treat it like a dare?

_____

Who is the chef, who is the eater, and is that sustainable?

_____

REFLECTION BOX:

Could I eat like this forever?" Is this cute now... but annoying by year three?" Does this person *respect* food or treat it like a dare?"

_____

_____

REVIEW BOX:

Food Preferences

Meal Planning

Leftovers

Household Chores

Loading the Dishwasher

Grocery Shopping

Paper Towels Usage

She cooks... he "seasons" things off of TikTok not

He eats everything burning-hot in temperature; he

Kitchen "Kaos

Cooking - To one cooking is the same as high school

Food Doneness

Name brand loyalty

Eating at the table

Using plates

Cleaning as you cook vs tornado kitchen aftermath

Saving vs Throwing Away plastic Containers

Cooking Frequency

Table Eater

Spice Tolerance
Refrigerator Logic

Seasoning Style

Cooking Style: Chef vs Chaos

Meal Plan vs Wing It

MONEY, BILLS & WHY IS AMAZON HERE AGAIN?

Budgeting styles: saver, spender, or faith-based shopping? Love is spiritual, but so is debt.

Gift-Giving Style

- Thoughtful, sentimental gifts vs "I just Venmo'd you some money."
- One embarrasses the other by giving cheap gifts to family and friends of occasions and holidays.

Holiday Gift Spending

- Budgeted and thoughtful vs YOLO swipe the credit card.

Random Purchases

- Minimalist vs "Amazon package every day."

Careful, this could be a dealbreaker.

When Jalen and Priya first started dating, money wasn't an issue. They split frappuccinos, shared appetizers, and agreed that "life is about experiences, not material things."

Then they moved in together.

Day 3:

A mysterious Amazon box appeared on the porch. Then another. Then four more. Priya asked, "Did you order something?"
Jalen said, "Not really... just a few things."
A *few* things turned out to be:

- a drone,
- three hoodies,
- a mini projector,
- and a samurai sword "because it was 60% off."

Priya asks, "Did we *need* this?"

Jalen answers, "Need is a strong word."

Day 10:

Priya opened a spreadsheet labeled "Household Budget + Financial Projections." Jalen opened DoorDash because he "didn't feel like cooking... again."

Day 15:

She suggested saving for a home. He suggested crypto. That was the moment Priya realized: "We don't have money problems. We have *philosophical differences about money,* which is worse."

And that's when she also realized that when dining out that he didn't order but shared what she ordered to save money, even though he was making mid six figures per year. She hadn't even so much as enjoyed a full salad in a restaurant because he had to have not half, but most of it. Every time. Sometimes when she was still hungry, she would just order another salad. Then he would eat half of that. Priya now realized that this manis hungry. He won't let her eat a full meal--, but he will shop.

Big Purchases

- Researches, compares, budgets vs "I bought a jet ski — surprise!"

Why This Matters

Money doesn't just affect bills. It affects:

- Stress level
- Spending habits
- Lifestyle expectations
- How you feel about your partner's decisions
- Whether you wake up to a future… or a stack of monthly payments
- It expects power.

Buying $900 worth of "essentials" during a Target run will not strengthen the average marriage.

Love may be blind. Debt has 20/20 vision.

REAL COMPATIBILITY TRAPS: MONEY EDITION

Saver vs Spender

- One budgets every penny. The other says "I'll worry about it later," and later is now crying in overdraft fees.
- If one person saves, but the other YOLOs, your *couple-hood* escalates into a rescue mission.

Credit Score Reality Check

- One has an 812 credit score and color-coded files.
- The other says "I think my score starts with a 4?"
- Some people have credit. Some have vibes.

Bills on Auto-Pay vs 'I'll Get to It'

- One pays early.
- One gets emails that start with "FINAL NOTICE."
- Red flag: the lights go off… and they're not even panicked.

Big Purchases

- "Let's research and compare options."
- "I bought a jet ski."

Marriage is teamwork. Impulse buying is solo energy.

Food Budget vs Takeout Life
One can feed a family for $40/week.

- The other spends $40 on a smoothie and avocado toast.
- Expensive toast can make a budget *toast*.

Elitist or Salvage Barn Shopping?

Sales & Coupons vs Luxury Brands Only. One waits for discounts. The other says "Full price = self-worth."

One of y'all is building a future. The other is building an aesthetic.

Lending Money to Family

- "We help family when they need it."
- "No. Absolutely not. We are not a bank."
- You're not just marrying a person. You're marrying how they treat *their people.* Eventually, your spouse's karma may affect you.

Money Lending & Family Boundaries

- One loans money to relatives.
- The other is "absolutely not."
- The other who is absolutely not uses you for the scapegoat.

Relatives?

- One has no lines between themselves and their childhood relatives. What's mine is yours. After marriage if that turns into, "what is my spouse's is also yours".... <u>Have you two talked about this?</u>

- The other has grown up and individuated and cleaved to their spouse when they got married.

Relatives? *(Yes, them again.)*

- One lets their relatives do anything, borrow anything, use anything take anything – no boundaries.

Many years ago (in high school) I made matching shirts for myself and my then-boyfriend. Two weeks later I was at his parents' house wearing my matching shirt. To my shock, I saw his brother wearing the shirt. Why would I want a matching shirt with his brother? And it was his older brother, not a kid brother.

- The other has firm boundaries. I guess I'm the boundary person.

Future Planning

- One has a retirement plan and investments.
  The other thinks "manifesting abundance" *is* a retirement plan.
- Vision boards do not substitute for deposits.

Subscription Awareness

- One tracks every membership. The other has been paying for Hulu, Spotify, Crunchyroll, Audible, and a gym they haven't entered since 2021.

What Counts as "Emergency" Money

- Car repair, dental bill, medical cost
- My favorite band announced a tour, this IS an emergency"
- You will learn their true priorities real quick.

A Borrower or a Lender?

- Does your person mooch off of others, and you don't even know anything about it? Unknown to you, do they owe people money, and that's why your friend circle is getting thin?
- Do they spend, lend, share money indiscriminately – *"for all my friends"* buying rounds at the bar?

Financial Style

- One budgets down to the penny.
- The other just spends the pennies.

BEFORE YOU GET MARRIED, ASK:

If we had $10,000 extra right now, how would *they* want to spend it? Would they want to spend it? All? Save some? Save all?

Does my person make me feel secure… or stressed?

Am I prepared to share a budget with my person AND their impulses?

☐ Yes

☐ No

☐ I'll just pray and hope for the best (not recommended)

- The other believes
  I deserve this, and "future me will figure it out."

REVIEW BOX:

Gift-Giving Style

Holiday Gift Spending

Random Purchases

Big Purchases

Saver vs Spender

Credit Score Reality Check
Bills on Auto-Pay vs 'I'll Get to It'

Big Purchases

Food Budget vs Takeout Life

Elitist or Salvage Barn Shopping?

Lending Money to Family

Money Lending & Family Boundaries

Relatives?

Relatives? *(Yes, them again.)*

Future Planning

Subscription Awareness

What Counts as "Emergency" Money

A Borrower or a Lender?

Financial Style

BATHROOM & HYGIENE REALITIES

"You don't know someone until you share a bathroom."

When Kayla and Andre were dating, everything smelled like vanilla, cocoa butter, and romance. Then they spent one full weekend *sharing* a bathroom.

Day 1:
Kayla opened the shower and found 13 empty shampoo bottles lined up like a memorial for products long deceased. Andre said, "I don't throw them out until I'm *sure* they're empty."

Day 2:
Andre couldn't find his toothbrush.
Kayla said, "It's in the holder."
Andre said, "Which one? There are SEVEN."
Kayla said, "They're all mine. They have moods."

Day 3:
Kayla went to brush her teeth. The toothpaste was gone. She couldn't find it anywhere. An hour later she found it in the shower. Okay, now she sees that the cap to the toothpaste tube is gone — just gone. The toothpaste was like caulk or cement – it wouldn't come out. The tube looked like it had been squeezed by a toddler going

through something emotional. Andre said, "It still works, doesn't it?"

Day 4:
Andre opened the cabinet and quietly whispered, "Why does she have five different face creams… and they all say 'night?'"

Day 5: His bath towel smelled like it had survived a shipwreck. Then she wondered why she had put her nose up to it to smell it in the first place.

By day 6, Kayla had learned:

"Men and women don't share bathrooms--, well, at least not the same side of the bathroom—the same cabinets--, the same sink. They coexist inside a hygiene negotiation zone."

WHY THIS MATTERS

Bathrooms reveal who a person truly is:

- Are they clean or do they just *look* clean?
- Do they shower daily or believe in "natural oils?"
- Do they use one bar of soap for everything?
- Do they trim their nails *over the sink* like a villain?
- Do they leave hair in the drain like a DNA crime scene?

You can fake kindness. You cannot fake toothpaste discipline.

REAL COMPATIBILITY TRAPS: BATHROOM EDITION

Toothpaste Logic

- Squeezes from the bottom = civilized
- Squeezes from the middle = chaos coordinator
- Leaves the cap off = bathroom terrorist
- Uh, use your own toothbrush, please.

You're not just sharing a life. You're sharing *oral care values*.

Shower Frequency
One showers daily, or twice daily.
The other showers only "when needed." Ask them what "needed" means. Brace yourself.

Shower Length

In and out in 5 mins vs 45-minute steaming spa ritual waiting for the shower to turn into a steam shower or a sauna.

Smell Goods -One douses in fragrance, perfume, cologne, body sprays, powders and oils. The other just wants soap.

Towel Usage
One towel per shower vs four or five.

One towel per week; no exceptions vs Why can't I have a fresh towel today?.

If the towel smells like regret, run.

Hair in the Drain
One cleans the drain every time.
The other leaves behind enough DNA to clone themselves.

Shaving Residue

- Rinses and wipes the sink
- Leaves beard hair sprinkled like paprika
- Nothing says "romance is dead" like sink stubble.

Number of Products

- One bottle, labeled "Body/Hair/Car/Windows"
- 47 bottles, each with a specific function, scent, season, and emotional purpose

Neither is wrong. They are just... different species.

Sharing Bathroom Counter Space

- Toothbrush + floss vs entire Sephora display.

Dusty Ankles

- Beauty& Grooming Regimens – one doesn't understand why the other has to primp or preen for so long...
- The other doesn't understand why their spouse spends no time on grooming,.. look at those dry, ashy, dusty ankles.

Mirror Etiquette

- Wipes the fog and splatter
- Leaves toothpaste freckles

A bathroom mirror is a relationship mirror. Believe that.

Bathroom Fan Usage

One turns it on for 30 minutes.
The other unleashes toxic injustice and walks away like nothing happened.

If they don't respect air… they don't respect YOU.

Toilet Paper Roll Behavior

Replaces it like a responsible adult

Leaves the sad cardboard tube like a monument to laziness

OR puts a new roll *on top* — the laziest act known to mankind

Toilet Paper Orientation

Over. Under. Or "just sitting on top of the empty roll like a monster." FYI, under makes the paper unroll very easily, due to gravity and causes a lot of wastage, (no pun intended).

Gotta *Use It*?

- Wants privacy; shuts the door.
- Never shuts any door and all bathroom sounds, smells, and activities are for all to experience.

One is a Flusher and the other, not so much? Better sort this out sooner than later.

Toilet Seat Culture
One always puts it down.
The other thinks gravity is "strong enough to handle it."

If you hear a splash at 3am, it's already too late.

Bathroom Etiquette

- One thinks you cannot step on the bathmat after the shower because then the mat would get wet.
- Isn't that what it's for?
- One wants four towels per shower.
- One uses a towel once per shower, leaves it on the floor as if the house is a hotel with maid service.
- The other will use the same towel for a month if you don't take it from them.

BEFORE YOU GET MARRIED, ASK:

Could I look at their bathroom habits every day and still feel attracted to them?

☐ Yes
☐ No
☐ Not without counseling and disinfectant wipes

Whose hygiene style is "normal," and whose is a lawsuit?

Do I love this person… or do I just love them fully clothed, far from a shared sink?

You don't know a person until you've seen how they treat the toothpaste tube

Toothpaste Logic

Shower Frequency

Shower Length

One douses in fragrance

Towel Usage
Hair in the Drain
Shaving Residue

Number of Products

Sharing Bathroom Counter Space

Beauty& Grooming Regimens -Dusty Ankles

Mirror Etiquette

Bathroom Fan Usage
Toilet Paper Roll Behavior

Toilet Paper Orientation

Gotta *Use It*?

One is a Flusher and the other, not so much

Toilet Seat Culture

Bathroom Etiquette

DRIVING, ERRANDS & TRAVEL and CAR HABITS

Road trip or break-up trip?

You should be able to ride in a car together. *Right*?

When Evan offered to drive Mia to brunch on their third date, she thought it was sweet. He even opened the car door for her. A gentleman. Points awarded.

Then… he started driving. Mia discovered 3 things fast:

- He treats every yellow light like a dare from God.
- He will yell at other drivers as if they can hear him through the glass, the wind, and common sense.
- His blinker is *decorative.*
- *He uses the turn signals (blinkers)more when playing Grand Theft Auto, than in real life.*

Meanwhile, Evan discovered 3 things about Mia:

- She hits the invisible brake on the passenger side every 7 seconds.

- She gasps out loud at normal lane changes like they just avoided a fiery death.
- She turns the radio down when she's stressed — as if silence will stop a collision.

Then they took their first weekend road trip together, and more truths surfaced:

- She wanted to stop every 90 minutes "just to stretch."
- He thought stopping was "a sign of weakness," and frankly, a waste of time. He had this trip fully scheduled.
- She packed snacks, wipes, water, and Advil.
- He brought vibes.

The breaking point? He wanted to beat the traffic and arrive early. She wasn't ready to leave on time. They arrived… *never.* That was the day Mia realized:

> You're not just dating someone, you're dating their driving style, road rage level, time management skills, and relationship with gas stations.

Car Cleanliness

- One has a car that smells like pine and progress.
- The other has 14 water bottles, receipts from 2021, rolling around on the floor beneath your feet, and melted Skittles fused to the seat.

- *If the car is the owner's food journal in real time—worry.*
- Philosophy differences: My car is my sanctuary, or My car is a trashcan with wheels.

Full of Gas?

Leaves no gas in the car vs. Fills the car tank every trip—can't go to the store 2 miles away unless the tank is full. Just in case.

Maintenance vs Repair

- Fixes things early vs waits till the house smoke alarm is literally smoking.
- Do the smoke detectors even detect anything anymore?
- Thinks check engines lights on the dashboard are holiday decorations.
- Takes the vehicle(s) in for regular service vs. expects you to take the vehicle(s) in every time because your time is not as important as theirs.
- If the family's safety is not guarded – can you live with that?

Taking Phone Calls in the Car

- Uses Bluetooth vs speakerphone on max volume.

Driving Rules--, what rules? You mean, there are rules to driving on the road? I only needed the rules to get the license, now that I have it, I can do anything I want. *Right?*

- One drives calmly.
- The other has "road rage with a playlist."

Someone once asked me why I was driving so slowly. I responded, well it's an expensive car, and it's yours, so I can't let you know what I'd really do with this machine with you present.

In the car -One wants silence while the other wants to talk.

Music Volume in the Car

- Quiet background vs full concert experience—sometimes to avoid talking or real communication.

Holding Hands? Don't touch me, I'm driving.

You Can't Eat in My Car vs the other getting snacks for the road trip.

Driving Chaos

- One wants to look at the telephone, text, and select the playlist while driving--, not **_at_** the stop light, **while** driving. The other has slid out of their seat and is on the floor in morbid fear, bracing for impact. Every stop is inches away from the car in front.
- The other stops three car lengths away from the next car ahead, just to be safe.

Trent and Edie flew to Savannah to buy a car that Trent saw online and just had to have. Edie thought it would be an adventure, so she agreed. They would drive the car back to Virginia. It would be a real road trip and an adventure. Right after the car was purchased Trent proudly took the wheel, but he hated the car immediately. Trent said the car kept pulling and he felt like he didn't have control of it. It was such a jerky ride whereas that brand of car was known for a smooth ride.

Edie noticed it too, the car kept beeping like something was wrong. Terrence kept complaining, so Edie suggested, we should turn around and take this back, it might be a lemon.

Trent didn't want to take the car back, but he was exasperated with it, so he told Edie to drive. When Edie drove, there was no pulling or beeping. Finally, Edie realized what was happening and told Trent. When Trent drives, he is all over the lane they were supposed to be in. The car was putting Trent back in the lane – the car had lane assist. Trent is such a bad driver that he doesn't stay in the lane he should be in. Like ever. It took the car to tell him, because he would never listen to Edie.

One day Trent announced that he wanted to get a boat. Heck to the no! Edie thought to herself, as bad as he drives on dry ground, I am not getting on a boat with him at the helm. Trent and Edie ended up breaking up over something else, but after their breakup Edie realized that she had PTSD from Trent's driving. It was that bad.

Left Lane Driving t

- One drives as fast as possible like it's the Autobahn.
- The other is in the left lane going 20 miles under the speed limit—just to be safe.

Drives with purpose vs goes 45mph in the passing lane.

Use of Blinker While Driving

- Law-abiding adult vs "my lane change is *intuitive*—forgot that the signal light package came standard with the vehicle.

WHY ALL THIS MATTERS

Nothing exposes a person faster than:

- Being trapped together in a vehicle
- Seeing how they treat strangers on the road
- Watching them ignore the gas light
- Learning whether they respect stop signs or treat them as suggestions from the government

Also:

- Errands reveal patience
- Road trips reveal rhythm
- Airports reveal sanity

If you can't survive a Costco run together, a marriage license won't fix that.

- And it matters most because: **PTSD IS REAL**. There was less stress from the breakup than for how they drove trauma.

REAL COMPATIBILITY TRAPS: DRIVING & TRAVEL EDITION

Calm Driver vs Emotionally Unwell NASCAR Member

- One holds the wheel with peace. The other is yelling "USE YOUR BLINKER, DEMON" at a grandmother in a Honda.

Speed Limit Follower vs Speed Limit Philosopher Some people believe in 45 mph. Others believe the speed limit is a *suggestion for cowards.*

Gas Light Logic

- Fills up at half tank
- Waits until the car starts blinking like it's begging for its life. Drives on fumes that you can't even smell because there are not enough fumes to create a smell.
- Fuel anxiety or being broken down or stranded on the road is real stress.

Road Trip Style
One packs snacks, playlists, itinerary.
The other brings a dead phone and vibes.

Driving Music Compatibility

- "Let's listen to a podcast."
- "Let's listen to trap music at 7 a.m."

You'll learn who they really are by mile 14.

Talking During Driving
Driver: "Please don't talk to me while I'm merging."
Passenger: "So anyway, about your childhood trauma—"

Not all topics are highway-safe.

Navigation Trust Issues
One believes in GPS.
The other says "I know a shortcut," and then you end up in a field.

Airport Personality

- Arrives 2 hours early, documents boarding pass
- Arrives 14 minutes before takeoff and blames the universe

You can't fix that with love. That's wiring.

BEFORE YOU GET MARRIED, ASK:

Can I be in a moving vehicle with this person and feel safe, respected, and alive?

- [ ] Yes
- [ ] No
- [ ] Only if I drive every time

Who is the calm one, and who is the chaos one?

Could we take a 5-hour road trip together… and still want to speak afterward?

TRAVEL, DRIVING, & ERRANDS

(The "I didn't know you drove like that" category)

Car Cleanliness

Full of Gas?

Maintenance vs Repair & Safety

Taking Phone Calls in the Car

Driving Rules--, what rules?

In the car

Music Volume in the Car

Holding Hands?

You Can't Eat In My Car

Driving Chaos

Left Lane Driving

Drives with purpose

Calm Driver vs Emotionally Unwell NASCAR Member

Speed Limit Follower

Gas Light Logic

Car Cleanliness Philosophy

Road Trip Style

Driving Music Compatibility

Talking During Driving

Navigation Trust Issues

Airport Personality

•

PHONE, TECH, AND SOCIAL MEDIA BEHAVIOR

TV Remote Control Etiquette

- Volume police vs "turn it UP, I can't hear!"

Phone in Bed

- Scrolls all night vs puts it on silent across the room.

- The other doesn't call or text you back all day because they don't even know where their phone is or forgot to charge it up last night.

Phone at dinner or put away

Immediate texter vs delayed responder

Posting everything online vs private life

Speakerphone in public

Video games hours vs none Video Game / Screen Time

- Plays casually vs disappears into virtual world for 9 hours.

How they handle group chats

Tells friends/family about arguments or keeps private

FaceTime in the house vs headphones

Movie watching: silent vs commentary

- *Is this a relationship or a TikTok livestream?*

Phone Call Volume

- Whispery private calls vs full-speaker FaceTime in public.

These are things you need to know ahead of time so your life will work and also be enjoyable.

PHONE, TECH & SOCIAL MEDIA BEHAVIOR

Working title: "Is this a relationship or a livestream?"

"Is this a relationship or a livestream?"

Lila and Marcus had what looked like a perfect relationship — at least *online.*
They had couple selfies, matching filters, and a cute shared hashtag: #LoveLikeOurs.

But in real life? It's a different story.

First red flag: Date night, Lila lit candles. Set the table. Made dinner. Marcus says, genuinely, "Aww, this looks amazing. Hold on — don't touch anything yet. I need to take a picture." *15 minutes later, dinner was cold... but the photo got 172 likes.*

Second red flag: Every time they argued, Marcus posted vague quotes like:

"Funny how the people you care about hurt you the most."

Lila says, "BABY. WE ARE IN THE SAME HOUSE. Why are you sub tweeting me?"

Third red flag: Marcus took 47 selfies before leaving the house — but never once noticed Lila's new hair.

Fourth red flag: She found out he still had his dating apps… "but only for networking."
Networking with who, Marcus? The Lord?

That was the moment Lila realized:

Some people don't want a relationship. They want a co-star for their content—if that. If you have ever noticed on or off vacation they want you to take pictures of them, but you're not in the pix. They take pictures of scenery, but not of you. If you ask for a picture, or to be in one – it's only on your phone. Now that's **the red flag of all red flags.**

WHY THIS MATTERS

Phones are no longer just tools. They are:

- A distraction
- A coping mechanism

- A secret world
- A source of validation
- A private diary
- A public broadcast system
- A silent third partner in the relationship
- They can be an invasion.

You're not just dating a person. You're dating their screen time. You are competing with the world and the imagination of the world for their attention.

When you are with someone who lives in their phone… you'll always feel like you're interrupting them.

REAL COMPATIBILITY TRAPS: PHONE & TECH EDITION

Phone at Dinner vs Phone Away at Dinner
One is present.
The other is *digitally present in 5 other rooms, countries, and timelines.*

Poster vs Private
One documents every moment.
The other believes "not everything needs to be content."

If they post your arguments on Instagram stories, leave.

Speakerphone People
Some people take calls on speaker in public… loudly…

with no shame. This is not a compatibility issue. This is a humanitarian crisis.

Delayed Texter vs Instant Responder

- "Sorry, I just saw this."
- "You didn't answer my text from 12 seconds ago??"

Both are valid. Together? Chaos.

Scrolling at Bedtime

Some people put their phones away at night.
Some people scroll like they're trying to catch the internet before it expires.

Blue light is not romance.

Notification Personality

- 0 unread messages, inbox at zero
- 46,273 unread emails, and they're fine with it

If this gives you anxiety, pay attention.

Livestream Lifestyle

One lives life.
The other says, "Wait, don't eat yet, I need to film this for my followers."

One lives to create content the other to consume it.

Imagine explaining to your children that daddy went viral… but not to work.

Password Transparency

- "Here, hold my phone."
- "Why do you need my password?"

It's not about spying. It's about trust patterns.

Relationship Status: Posted or Private

One posts couple pics.
One posts quotes like "God is all I need."

If they're hiding you... they're advertising something.

Device Addiction

Some people live *with* technology.
Some people live *through* it.

You should not be competing with strangers on a screen.

BEFORE YOU GET MARRIED, ASK:

Do they treat me like a person... or a background character to their phone?

Can we enjoy silence without screens... or do we panic?

Is this love... or is this content?
- ☐ Love
- ☐ Content
- ☐ Both, but one of us needs therapy

REVIEW BOX:

TV Remote Control Etiquette

Phone in Bed

Phone at dinner or put away

Immediate texter vs delayed responder

Posting everything online vs private life

Speakerphone in public

Video games hours vs none

How they handle group chats

Tells friends/family about arguments or keeps private

FaceTime in the house vs headphones

Movie watching: silent vs commentary

Phone Call Volume

Phone at Dinner

Poster vs Private
Speakerphone People

Delayed Texter vs Instant Responder

Scrolling at Bedtime
Notification Personality

Livestream Lifestyle

Password Transparency

Relationship Status: Posted or Private
Device Addiction

COMMUNICATION & EMOTIONAL STYLE

Dealing with Stress

- Wants to talk it out vs goes completely silent.

How They Apologize

- Full ownership vs "sorry you feel that way."

(Where relationships actually rise or die)

- How they apologize
- Silent treatment vs talk it out
- Conflict timing: fix now vs cool-off period
- How they handle stress
- Need for affirmation vs independence
- Defensive vs reflective in arguments
- Blame-shifting vs ownership
- Needs reassurance vs "I told you once"
- Dramatic sighing vs calm processing

- Humor in conflict: helpful or hostile?
- *Silent treatment vs "we need to process this right now"*

"Silent treatment vs 'We're not sleeping until we fix this.'"

Aaliyah and Chris had never argued while dating. Not once. They took that as a sign they were "meant to be." Then came their first disagreement after becoming "official-official."

The issue? Something small, irrelevant, and dumb — like the correct way to load a dishwasher.
But it wasn't about the dishwasher.
It was about communication styles that revealed themselves like jump scares.

Aaliyah believed in talking things out immediately.
She grew up in a family where people had *family meetings over spilled juice.*

Chris believed in thinking silently for three to five business days before responding.
He came from a family where people communicated by slamming cabinet doors and sighing like ghosts with chest pain.

So during their first argument:

- Aaliyah said, "Let's talk about this now."
- Chris said, "I don't want to talk right now."

- Aaliyah heard: "I'm abandoning you emotionally."
- Chris heard: "You are not allowed to have space as a human."

Then Chris tried to walk away.
Aaliyah followed.
Chris walked faster.
Aaliyah followed faster.

He felt chased.
She felt ignored.

Nobody won.
Not even the dishwasher.

That was the day they both learned:

You don't need the same personality to stay in love.
But you DO need compatible communication defaults…
or arguments become full-time jobs.

Uses Sighing as a Weapon

- Normal breathing, and normal use of words in conversations vs dramatic exhale to express dissatisfaction without using words.

Who They Tell About Your Arguments

- Nobody.
- Their momma.
- Their friends and buddies.
- Their work-spouse.

- Their entire family group chat.
- Everybody.

How They End a Bad Day

- Talks it out vs disappears into silence, games, or bed.

WHY THIS MATTERS

You're not just marrying how someone talks. You're marrying:

- how they argue
- how they shut down
- how they apologize
- how they express stress
- how they handle conflict timing
- whether they need space or need resolution
- how emotional safety is created… or destroyed

Most couples don't fail because they *don't love each other*.
They fail because they don't know how to stay connected while disagreeing.

REAL COMPATIBILITY TRAPS: COMMUNICATION EDITION

Fight Now vs Fight Later
One says, "We resolve this tonight."
The other says, "Not talking for 72 hours seems healthy to me."

Time-outs help some people. They trigger others. Know which you are.

Silent Treatment vs Emotional Over-Talking

- One withdraws.
- One chases.

That's not romance, that's a Tom & Jerry episode.

Logic Fighter vs Feelings Fighter

- "Let's be rational."
- "Let's be real about how this *felt*."

If both want to "win," the relationship loses.

Apology Speed

- "I'm sorry, let's move on."
- "We're going to sit with this for 7 hours and analyze every word."

Apology Language

- "Sorry I hurt you."

- "Sorry you feel that way."

One is an apology. One is a gaslight in a cardigan.

Internal Processor vs Verbal Processor

- Needs time to think before speaking
- Needs to speak to *be able* to think

Compatibility is not sameness. It's rhythm.

Blame Thrower vs Accountability Taker
Some people apologize for their part.
Others say, "Well *you* always…" like a reflex.

Marriage counseling starts here.

Sarcasm vs Sensitivity
One roasts playfully.
The other gets emotionally wounded by tone alone.

You need a shared sense of humor or a shared therapist.

Feeling Seen vs Feeling Criticized
"Can you help me fix this?" vs "You're attacking me."

One person's suggestion is another person's personal injury lawsuit.

Conflict Energy

- Calm debater
- Emotional escalator

If someone shouts and someone shuts down, the relationship becomes a dead battery.

One seeks peace, one seeks understanding. Both matter.

BEFORE YOU GET MARRIED, ASK:

Can we disagree without destroying each other?
☐ Yes
☐ No
☐ TBD but it's giving "risk"

REFLECTION BOX:

Do I feel heard when we argue — or just exhausted?

_____

_____

Is our communication healthy, or are we just hoping marriage will magically fix.

_____

_____

REVIEW BOX:

Dealing with Stress

How They Apologize

Uses Sighing as a Weapon

Who They Tell About Your Arguments

How They End a Bad Day

Fight Now vs Fight Later

Silent Treatment

Logic Fighter

Apology Language

Internal Processor

Blame Thrower

Sarcasm vs Sensitivity

Feeling Seen vs Feeling Criticized

Conflict Energy

Apology Speed

How They Argue

How They Argue

"Let's fix this now" vs "give me three days."

One needs to go out every weekend.

The other wants home, blankets, and streaming forever.

CLOTHING & PERSONAL ITEMS

"Borrowing" Your Things

- Brings it back vs it disappears forever.
- Your favorite hoodie or T-shirt... etc.

Seasonal Clothing Swap

- Organized totes labeled by season vs "all clothes live in one pile, all year."

Does Your Person Ever throw things away or are they still wearing their outfits from junior high school?

Buys new clothes when necessary, vs that t-shirt from high school is my favorite and those underwear are still good; they only have one or two holes in them. Clothing Storage

Closet has hangers vs "pile at the end of bed is my system."

Takes up all the closet space vs. the other who is willing to share.

Clothes or shoes or handbag obsessions vs Clothes are clothes it doesn't matter the brand names.

Dryer Lint Trap

- Cleans it every cycle vs "You have to clean that?"

- Rushes to take the clothes from the dryer to hang or fold them vs. the other thinks the dryer is his sock drawer and leaves everything there until used.

Folding vs Stuffing Laundry

- Drawers look like retail store vs a closet that a tornado swept through.

- One folds everything neatly and puts things where they belong. The other cannot find anything that belongs to them, not their clothes, shoes, keys—and expects the organized person to find their things for them. Usually in a panic because they are late. Again.

Appropriateness: Knows what to wear, when. Hot pants and halters are not for the office. Gym clothes are for the gym, *buster*. We're going to a nice restaurant for my birthday.

BEFORE YOU GET MARRIED, ASK:

If you're moving into their house, have they made room for you?

Do you have the right to make any changes?

Do you have to sleep on the bed that they slept on with their ex?

_____

_____

REVIEW BOX:

"Borrowing" Your Things

Seasonal Clothing Swap

"Borrowing" Your Things

Seasonal Clothing Swap

Buys new clothes when necessary

Takes up all the closet space

Dryer Lint Trap

Folding vs Stuffing Laundry

Buys new clothes when necessary

Clothes, shoes, handbags obsession…

Takes up all the closet space

Appropriateness

PETS, KIDS, FAMILY & "OTHER HUMANS YOU DIDN'T MARRY"

Are you marrying them, or their whole bloodline and dog? Yes.

"You're not just marrying them — you're marrying their whole ecosystem."

When Serena started dating Leon, she thought she was dating one man. Tall, handsome, funny, great smile. Then... she met everything that came with him.

First: The Dog.

A 70-pound fur-covered roommate named Bentley, who:

- Slept in the bed *between* them
- Shed enough hair to knit sweaters for orphans
- Ate salmon but refused kibble
- Barked at air... and won

Leon said, "He was here first."
Serena said, "But not on my pillow, please."

Second: The Family.
Leon's mother called every day, sometimes twice a day.
His sister had a key to his apartment "just in case."
His cousin popped in randomly to "borrow" things he never returned.

Third: His Best Friend.
A man named Rico who:

- Called Leon at 11:30 p.m. to discuss life crises
- Had no filter
- Believed "bro code overrides romance"

Fourth: Children in the Future
Serena said she wanted 2 max.
Leon said 5 minimum. Bentley barked in agreement.

That was when Serena realized that you don't just marry a person, you marry their pets, their parents, their people, their patterns, and their future plans. And sometimes... their dog.

Pet Tolerance

- One treats the dog like a child.
- The other thinks "animals do NOT belong in the bed, or house for that matter. They are used to yard dogs."
- One would rather cuddle with the dog than their spouse vs You've got to be kidding me right now.

Pet Hair Tolerance

- Accepts it as part of life vs lint-rolls everything daily.

Kids & Discipline Style

- One is gentle parenting; or hardly any—the kids can do whatever.
- The other is "because I said so, and there are strict rules."

Relatives?

- One has no lines between themselves and their childhood relatives.
- The other has grown up and individuated and cleaved to their spouse when they got married.

Relatives? Again? YUP

- One lets their relatives (or friends) do anything, borrow anything, use anything, take anything – no boundaries.

It's heartbreaking to realize that the thing you got your person that matches yours and is designed to be something special between you two, didn't mean anything to them. Next thing you know, his friend Bob, or his cousin Sheila now has it or is wearing it.

- The other has firm boundaries. I guess I'm the boundary person.

WHY THIS MATTERS

You're not choosing a spouse You're choosing a permanent role in their social ecosystem.

That includes:

- The way they raise (or plan to raise) kids
- Their loyalty to family — healthy or dysfunctional
- Their loyalty to you and your relationship.
- How much their friends influence their decisions
- Whether pets are "cute companions" or "fur children with legal rights"
- Whether holidays are shared, rotated, or emotionally negotiated
- Whether they believe in boundaries — or *pretend* to

If you don't like their ecosystem now, marriage won't shrink it, It will move it into your house.

REAL COMPATIBILITY TRAPS: FAMILY, PET, & KID EDITION

Pet Culture Clash

- "Pets are family."
- "Pets are animals."

You're not just agreeing on a dog. You're agreeing on roles, space, and fur tolerance.

Kids vs No Kids

"I definitely want children someday" vs the other who absolutely doesn't.

You can compromise on pizza toppings, not parenthood.

How Many Kids

One imagines 1–2.
The other imagines a reality show.

That's not a difference. That's a *lifestyle fork in the road.*

Parenting Style

Gentle parenting vs "Because I said so."

If you can't agree on bedtime for a toddler, imagine what you won't agree on when they are a teenager. Imagine how they will see that you two "parents" are divided and they can run the show now..

Extended Family Boundaries

"My mom has a key, she can stop by anytime."

"Your mom needs an appointment and a 24-hr notice."

Love doesn't erase in-law chaos.

Friend Group Integration Some friends are healthy. Some friends are *still 19 emotionally.*

If they ask "Can my friend move in for a while?" RUN.

Babysitting Beliefs

- "Family will help with the kids."
- "Nobody is raising my child but me."

Expectations fail when not discussed.

Financial Boundaries with Family Some think "We help family, no matter what." Some think "We are not AT&T for cousins with bad decisions."

This one breaks marriages silently.

Culture + Tradition Marriage is not just two people. Sometimes it's two entire traditions, customs, and recipes that have spiritual meaning.

Love is sweet. Culture is complicated.

BEFORE YOU GET MARRIED, ASK:

Do I respect — and *actually like* — the people and beings attached to this person?

☐ Yes
☐ No
☐ I like the dog but not the mother

Are we aligned on kids, pets, family visits, holiday plans, and "who gets the spare key?"

Am I prepared to be part of this ecosystem… or do I just want the person alone?

PETS, KIDS, FAMILY & BOUNDARIES

(The extended relationship you didn't marry, but you did)

- Pets in bed vs pets on floor
- House is for adults vs kids/pets run free
- Parenting style: gentle vs strict
- Wants kids vs doesn't
- How they talk to / about your family
- Holiday travel obligations
- Babysitting other people's kids
- Lending money to relatives
- **Pet Tolerance**
- **Pet Hair Tolerance**
- Kids vs No Kids
- How Many Kids
- Parenting Style
- Extended Family Boundaries
- Friend Group Integration
- Babysitting Beliefs
- Financial Boundaries with Family

FREE TIME, ENERGY & LIFESTYLE PACE

One wants brunch and museums. The other wants couch and Netflix.

When Bella and Omar first got together, every date felt exciting. Adventure. Spontaneity. Cute outfits. Shared playlists. Matching energy. Then came something more important than romance:

A Saturday.

Bella woke up at 8:00 a.m., bright-eyed, in leggings, making a to-do list titled: "Brunch → Farmers Market → Flea Market → Art Pop-Up → Maybe Rock Climbing."

Omar woke up at 11:45 a.m., hair sideways, mumbling: "What's for breakfast? Or lunch? Or whatever meal this is?"

Bella says, "Let's get moving!"

Omar replies, sleepily, "Moving where? Why? For what?"

Her ideal weekend: outdoors, cute coffee, experiences, photos, people, sunlight. His ideal weekend: blanket, snacks, TV, darkness, stillness, minimal talking.

She was energized by activity. He was energized by silence. She called it *living*. He called it *resting*.

That was the day Bella learned that if your energies don't flow together, you're not dating a soulmate —you're dating a scheduling conflict.

Another couple, Steve and Barb were together for four years. She begged him to go outside, exercise, be active, finally she realized that he would not. He absolutely would not. So, she broke up with him, four years and 20 unwanted pounds later.

WHY THIS MATTERS

You don't just share a home; you share *time*. How someone uses their free time tells you:

- Their priorities
- Their social battery
- How they recharge
- How much they need people vs peace
- Whether you'll live in two different rhythms under the same roof

You can love someone and still not *like* how they live.

REAL COMPATIBILITY TRAPS: FREE TIME & LIFESTYLE EDITION

Homebody vs Explorer

- "Let's stay in."
- "Let's go out."

If every weekend turns into a hostage negotiation, take note.

- Social Battery Levels
- One is drained by people.
- One *needs* social interaction to feel alive.

You can't go out every night *or* stay in every night. Somebody will resent somebody.

Weekend Intentions

- "Weekends are for recovery."
- "Weekends are for living before Monday kills us again."

Energy matters more than romance.

Hobby Compatibility

- One has no hobbies.
- One has 14 hobbies that require gear, fees, and emotional support.
- One reads, meditates, prays, writes vs the other who has a rock band that practices at the house every weekend.

A partner is not a hobby. A hobby is not a partner.

Event vs Solitude Preference

- Concerts, birthdays, weddings, clubs
- Reading, plants, naps, quiet

Both are valid. Opposites can work... unless they *never* overlap. Every time you go somewhere the other is impatient and ready to leave early or as soon as possible.

Fitness Lifestyle Gym 5x a week vs "my exercise is walking from couch to fridge."

Not a deal-breaker... until health, habits, or body image enters the chat.

Spontaneous vs Scheduled

- "Let's go now!"
- "I need 3–5 business days' notice to leave the house."

Your shared life will either feel exciting or exhausting.

Vacation Personality - Relaxing beach napper vs 6-city itinerary power tourist.

If one of you needs a vacation from the *vacation*, there might be a rhythm problem.

Seasonal Expectations One celebrates fall like a Pinterest board. One says "it's just weather."

You will witness emotional weather too. You exciting people, make sure your partner is not depressed. Also make sure you haven't hooked up with them as a project, to 'bring them out of their shell.' They may like their shell just fine.

Shared vs Separate Recharge Time If one person recharges *with* you and the other recharges *away* from you… prepare for misinterpretation, pouting, or "you don't want to be around me?"

BEFORE YOU GET MARRIED, ASK:

Do our energy levels match enough that we can build a life — not just a vibe?

☐ Yes

☐ No

☐ Only if we get separate calendars

Do I like how they spend free time?

Seasonal Decor

- One decorates for EVERY holiday, including Groundhog Day.
- The other says "why are there pumpkins in July?"

…or do I just tolerate it because we're in the honeymoon phase?

REFLECTION BOX:

If we had 48 free hours together… would that feel exciting or suffocating?

If my person suggested a road trip, would that feel exciting or scary?

Holiday Traditions

- One decorates in September.
- The other is "please don't put the tree up until December 24th."
- One wants the tree to stay up until March, the other wants to take it down on December 25, at dusk.
- One doesn't want any decorations whatsoever and the other thinks they are a total Grinch.

Visitors in the House

- One loves hosting.
- The other thinks people should leave after one hour, max.

Holiday Travel Obligations

- Visits both families vs "I'm not leaving my house."

Holiday Expectations

- One says "We spend Thanksgiving with my family."
- Other says "We rotate holidays fairly."
- Prepare for emotional drafts, guilt trips, and passive-aggressive casserole.
- Two solutions: Go to the one you want to be at the least – first. This way you have your built in excuse to leave.
- The other solution, if you want to be at both houses go on the EVE of the holiday to one and the actual holiday with the other. Rotate. All parents will usually be content with that.
- Third solution, ask one family to host a brunch and then take the main meal at the other family's house.

You're welcome.

Free Time

- Quiet hobbies vs constant activities.

Talking During Movies

- Silent immersion vs live commentary + 47 questions.

Three-Day Weekend Style

- "Let's rest" vs "Let's repaint the bathroom and take a road trip to three states."

Vacations – Watch for the 'I will never' vows that your person may have made that you don't know anything about – unless you ask.

- Relaxing resort vs 10-city itinerary with 6am wake-ups.
- I will not fly.
- I will not cruise.
- I will go east west or south, but never north—there's just too much traffic, and too many people.

LIFESTYLE & HOBBIES

(The weird stuff you don't find out until year three)

Crafts and things: one says it's a hobby, the other sees it as junk all over the place. This is more than an issue of tolerance, it is an issue of respect.

Left brain vs right brain. The artistic, crafty person is right brained, everything in order is the left brain. They can get along. They can marry. They can live together and be happy, as long as they respect one another.

REVIEW BOX:

Homebody vs Explorer

Weekend Intentions

Hobby Compatibility

Event vs Solitude Preference

Fitness Lifestyle

Spontaneous vs Scheduled

Vacation Personality

Seasonal Expectations

Shared vs Separate Recharge

Seasonal Decor

Holiday Traditions

Visitors in the House

Holiday Travel Obligations

Holiday Expectations

How They Spend Free Time

Talking During Movies

Three-Day Weekend Style

Vacation

THE 12 STEPS TO OUT THE DOOR, DUDE: CHEATING

The cheating scale no one agrees on — until it's too late.

Privacy vs Transparency

- One shares passwords.
- The other says "my phone is my phone."

Yes — every couple *thinks* they agree on cheating …until they actually define it. Some think cheating = only physical sex. Some think emotional closeness counts. Some think flirting is harmless. Some think "it doesn't count if nothing happened." Some think "if I have to hide it from you, it's cheating."

Old school, new school, and the cheating no one saw coming. "Everyone swears they know what cheating is… until they see the 12-level scale and realize they only agree on 2 of them."

Serious underestimation:

Flirting

- One is a constant flirt and will even do it in front of you vs the other is very respectful when with their partner.
- One will gawk at another attractive person, the other would never disrespect the person they are with.

"If I turn my head to not see you checking her up and down, it's because it hurts me, not because I didn't see it. Like a solar eclipse, I didn't want to look at it head on. This is not permission to do it again or to keep doing it. My head turn is pain, like a little vomit in the back of my throat, worse than the worst cramps or labor pain, but emotional. It's like the most severe form of heartburn.

Don't think I didn't see it or that you got away with it. That was me giving you Grace and it cost me a lot."

LEVEL 1 — *Suspicious But Defensible*

☐ Likes
☐ Harmless follows
☐ Old flirty texts not deleted

LEVEL 2 — *Digital Flirting / Attention-Seeking*

- ☐ Flirty comments
- ☐ Emojis with intent 😏
- ☐ "Thirst trap" behavior

LEVEL 3 — *Secret Texting / Deleted Messages*

- ☐ Hiding chats
- ☐ Locking phone
- ☐ "You're overreacting" defense

LEVEL 4 — *Emotional Cheating*

- ☐ Sharing deeper feelings
- ☐ Going to someone else for emotional comfort
- ☐ Talking like you're single

LEVEL 5 — *Secret Meetups*

- ☐ "It was just lunch"
- ☐ Not telling your partner
- ☐ One-on-one time that feels like a date

LEVEL 6 — *Porn / OnlyFans / Paid Content*

☐ Paying for sexual access
☐ Private subscriptions
☐ "It's not a real person" arguments

LEVEL 7 — *Sexting / Explicit Pics*

☐ Sending or receiving sexual images
☐ Dirty talk
☐ Screenshots = relationship over

LEVEL 8 — *Physical Flirting / Touching*

☐ Lap sitting
☐ Waist grabbing
☐ Touch with intention

LEVEL 9 — *Making Out / Partial Physical Cheating*

☐ Kissing
☐ Handsy behavior
☐ "It didn't go that far" excuse

LEVEL 10 — *Sexual Contact (Not Intercourse)*

☐ Spoken
☐ Sexual touching
☐ All the things people pretend "don't count"

LEVEL 11 — *Full Sexual Interaction*

☐ 100% cheating
☐ No loopholes

LEVEL 12 — *Artificial or Replacement Intimacy Cheating*

☐ AI girlfriend / AI boyfriend apps
☐ "Work wife" / "work husband" emotional bond
☐ Creating a fantasy relationship to escape your real one
☐ "It's not cheating because they're not real"
☐ Digital devotion that replaces true intimacy

This level is the *silent destroyer.*
No one touches anyone — but emotional loyalty is gone.

Lousy excuses like hall passes or I'm out with the boys or we are in another zip code, so it doesn't count won't fly.

REVIEW BOX:

This may be the hardest question of this entire book:

Can you have friends? I mean friends of your same gender, or will your person hit on all you friends? If that answer is yes, you have a way worse problem than compatibility.

LEVEL 1 — *Suspicious But Defensible*

LEVEL 2 — *Digital Flirting / Attention-Seeking*

LEVEL 3 — *Secret Texting / Deleted Messages*

LEVEL 4 — *Emotional Cheating*

LEVEL 5 — *Secret Meetups*

LEVEL 6 — *Porn / OnlyFans / Paid Content*

LEVEL 7 — *Sexting / Explicit Pics*

LEVEL 8 — *Physical Flirting / Touching*

LEVEL 9 — *Making Out / Partial Physical Cheating*

LEVEL 10 — *Sexual Contact (Not Intercourse)*

LEVEL 11 — *Full Sexual Interaction*

LEVEL 12 — *Artificial or Replacement Intimacy Cheating*

WORK

They say when you do what you love you'll never work a day in your life.

I say: Be sure you're getting paid while you're doing what you love—so you can live.

If you want to fish all day, then become a commercial fisherman.

Stephanie married a man who had not missed a day from work in the 12 years he had been working for the bank--, not even a sick day. I less than a year after marriage he quit his whole job because he feared that a woman was going to be promoted to be his boss. That did not happen, and yet he was basically a newlywed and jobless, leaving his wife as the solo breadwinner for the family.

Will your spouse work? That has already been decided, *right*? Is it a real job, a real career? Or, is sit a fantasy gig?

Livestream Lifestyle

- One lives life.
  The other says, "Wait, don't eat yet, I need to film this for my followers."

- One lives to create content the other to consume it.
- Imagine you ancestors—hunters who stopped to take a picture of that dinner in the wild instead of releasing that arrow from the bow to capture the meal.
- Imagine explaining to your children that daddy went viral… but not to work.

Can They **Keep** A Job?

Punctuality for Work/Appointments

- Shows up early and prepared vs running in sweating at the last second.

Ambition: Are they Ambitious

Are you?

Sick Days

- One wants nurturing.
- The other turns into a dramatic Victorian patient on their deathbed. This is often known as a man-cold.

How They Handle Being Late

- One leaves early.
- The other starts ironing clothes five minutes before departure. Late everywhere.

What Counts as 'On Time'

- 10 minutes early vs "if we're only 20 minutes late, that's fine."

Talking While the Other is Working

- Constant random chatter vs "please let me focus."

Obsessed With Work? All they talk about, all they think about and work calls all weekend? Are they a doctor, electrician, or emergency plumber? If not, is that okay?

Pay Day -do you know when that is? Do you have to know? You've discussed this, *right*?

Work Friends who may be wild and single. Are we okay with that?

Does your person have to go out with their 'work friends' several days a week after work?

Single friends – are the work friends single? Does that bother you?

Work Spouse? Are you okay with that?

Early Arriver vs **"We'll Get There When We Get There"** One says: "Let's leave at 8."Other says: "8 is a feeling, not a time." Or, "The cool people don't get there until 10."

BEFORE YOU GET MARRIED, ASK:

A fellow was trying to impress a girl one day and said that if she would be his girlfriend, he would go to work every day. So many questions, foremost, does this grown man not work, currently? These are telling and dangerous statements.

If you or your person both need to work to have a proper lifestyle then check their history to make sure, they are a viable candidate for you. Don't settle on their potential unless you are both ins school and haven't started working yet.

REVIEW BOX:

Can They Keep A Job?

Punctuality for Work/Appointments

Ambition: Are they Ambitious

Sick Days

How They Handle Being Late

What Counts as 'On Time'

Talking While the Other is Working

Obsessed With Work

Pay Day

Work Friends

Single friends

Work Spouse

Early Arriver vs "We'll Get There When We Get There

CAN I LIVE WITH THIS?

"Can I Live With This For the next 75 Years?" *may* not be the only marriage question, although it is important. In the dynamic of being very different from one another in the house and in the way of doing things, there may be struggles. It's not just about watching the other do things their way and your spouse watching you do things your way and both of you shaking your heads. No, battles may start. Battles may escalate. Wars may happen because if one or either of you is strong-willed and you may want to change your person.

How anyone does anything, especially how they live is not a matter necessarily of upbringing. Two can be brought up in the same house and do things completely different from one another. Twins can be totally different. One kid likes to play alone, the other kid wants a group play date all the time. One kid could be neat and organized and love to put their toys away, the other would rather leave toys as floor art and cry every day when they step on a Lego, but ever learn from it.

So, it's now a matter of how much grace you give your housemate to live the way they live. The next is how much, if any Grace, do they give you? And if you each do things completely differently, its not just how much they get on your nerves or vice versa, it is how does that affect the house?

In a business, for example, there are systems—this is done this way, that is done that way. Systems make things work, work efficiently, work for everyone, and it means the next person can jump right in where the last person left off because they understand the system. Now when a husband and wife procreate all of these differences that have not been settled or agreed upon will escalate in the child and confuse the child because how do you do dishes, mom, with a sponge or a dishcloth?

Incompatibility then becomes confusion. That's a bigger risk than two bickering about ways, means, and systems.

People love to say, "Marriage is hard." I'll tell you now that college is not hard--, it's a lot. College is a discipline and it takes discipline. Marriage, like college--, **relationship college** -- doesn't have to be hard, but it is daily. It's a lot; it takes discipline and created discipline. Now who disciples who is up to Wisdom and Grace in the union. Perhaps you both help and sharpen each other; it is not just one way or the highway. If you don't learn something new and a new way of doing things daily, then are you still living? One wise person said that when you stop learning, that is when you start aging.

Well.

So, marriage is not the wedding, the pictures, the reception or the honeymoon. It's not the Instagram announcement or the matching robes or the hash tagged vacation photos.

Marriage is learning to live together with knowledge. She likes this temperature so he will just wear this light sweater in the house or thicker pj's at night. He likes this temperature, so she can take off the sweatsuit and wear lighter fabrics. They can still be in love and also get along. The one who is always cold can check the iron levels in their blood. The one who is always hot might be running a low-grade fever or their BP might be high. There could be medical reasons for physiologic things. But look at the beauty of this, if both were single and never lived together, neither would have known to check these things. Two are better than one because two have a good reward, and that reward is evident when there is Grace and Love present. That reward is: I'm checking on you. Are you okay?

10,000 shared meals, some seasoned… some traumatizing and there is company at the dinner table, so if one chokes, the other knows the Heimlich maneuver, or at least hit you on the back real hard until you cough up whatever went down the wrong "pipe." Or, to get the other to the ER so they can assemble the gastroenterologist on call and muster the team to have that chunk of steak dislodged so they can breathe again.

Marriage is good. And those who learn how to make it work for them are very wise and will be rewarded very well in life.

It's not just 3,000 arguments about "what's wrong?" followed by "nothing." It's learning how to communicate with one another because you trust that the other person is not going to go off on you for telling the truth.

It could be 7,000 Sunday mornings of "who moves first or we'll both be late."

It could be toothpaste cap off—dried up toothpaste, dog hair, phone brightness at night, and loud TV's—and if you're lucky you say to yourself, well, I love them and that's the way this is.

Love starts it. Truth propels it. Grace soothes it. Compatibility keeps it alive.

THE DANGEROUS MYTH

We were raised to believe that romantic love is stronger than habits, rhythms, quirks, backgrounds, and defaults. It can be for a while – for the person who is waiting for the other person to "change." But more than romantic love is needed to conquer this. Wisdom – choose your battles. Agape love encompasses Wisdom, Grace, Truth and patience – it encompasses all so it conquers all.

But it must be two-sided for all that conquering.

And Grace, because they are human and you are human, do the extra things for one another. Love is the spark. Compatibility is the wiring. Wisdom, Grace, Truth are the electricity that flows to keep things going, flowing, and strong and the voltage levels even and safe.

A HEALTHY MARRIAGE IS NOT:

- Two perfect people
- Two identical people
- Two people who never disagree

It is two self-aware adults who know their own faults, who can communicate without cruelty, who can adjust, compromise, or at least *respect* each other's differences. The two do not treat marriage like a personality rehab program, or treat the spouse like an acquisition to be managed.

IMPORTANT TRUTH

You marry potential only if the other person has agreed to let you coach them. For example, Margie married Lou with them both knowing that Lou was going to law school after one year of marriage. Those would definitely be changes that Lou would agree to. Margie was already a lawyer.

Don't count on them changing. You can't even count on yourself to change, not really. But know this: when it comes to daily life, whatever they do now —they will do *more* of when they're comfortable, tired, overwhelmed, or unfiltered. If they won't change it while they're trying to impress you, they will not change it when they're searching for matching socks and personal peace.

For marriage to succeed, yes two need to be in love, but they need to respect one another as well. Men, especially need to be respected. A marriage can fail if two never learned to live together with respect, rhythm, humor, and reality. Neither can nag or be on the other's "case" all the time, that will run the other away.

Compatibility is required; it's either there naturally, or it can be learned. Neither in a marriage should be so rigid that they can't compromise on a few things from time to time. "Baby, the kitchen is yours, we will run it the way you say." Sweetie, she may say, "I will not try to rearrange the garage and if I get something like a hammer from it, I will put it back where you had it. I respect your system."

If you're not married yet, you have the gift of the knowledge in this book: Use it wisely. Really get to know your partner; don't be so starry-eyed that you don't see that they are throwing chicken bones on the floor of the car or out the window for that matter, if that bothers you. Heck, both of you could be throwing chicken bones out the window for all I know or care – you're out in the country, you feel hillbilly-ish, or you think you're not in the city right now and it's biodegradable. But if things bother you, deal with them as soon as.

Learn how to deal with things, do not argue, pick, nag, criticize. First observe; if it's a pattern then address it. You might play a game and say, "I really want us to get along when we are married, so you can tell me one thing that I do that you don't fully understand or wish I could change and I'll do the same. Maybe we'll do one a week until we sort things out. Ask real questions. Answer real questions when they are asked of you. You're not perfect. Study daily life, not just date-night life. Pay attention to the small things — they become the big things. Don't think that just because you love them so much these things won't bother you. Don't think that just because they love you so much that they will change. They may *even* want to change but may not be able to if their way of life is deeply engrained in them; and vice versa..

And remember, their folks will come over and maybe stay over sometimes and they will act just like them and may even wonder what's wrong with you. It's okay, right? You can bear it? Right—it's just a visit. But they haven't been through the intensive 'getting to know one another" course that the two of you have taken ourself through.

Worse, what if they do more than visit and move in with you all? Now it's not one, but it's two or more acting just like your spouse, amplifying it--, it's a matter of upbringing and these in-laws are the ones who raised this person you're married to. Eating dinner and tooth picking or sucking their teeth at the table after dinner. Worse, flossing at the dinner table, you will clearly see what is okay from their childhood homes, and if all are not careful, your spouse could fall right back into those childhood hillbilly patterns.

See. Know. Think all of this all the way through. No one is perfect, but if you are going to freak out at any of the things that you consider couth, manners, or proper upbringing, then brace yourself. What you think it normal might just be idiosyncrasies, so don't set yourself up to freak out. If you are the one who is quirky and causing your significant other to freak out, this book might be a good time for you two to have a meeting of the minds and see if and where you can compromise.

"Forever" sounds romantic but be sure that you can choose someone you can love *and live with*.

BEFORE YOU CLOSE THIS BOOK

If you're still with your person after reading all these chapters and you're still smiling? Congrats — you may just be ready.

Work it out. If it is workable, work it out; be married and be happy. Be sure to pray—some red flags are for your good and to stop you. I heard a speaker recently say that 80% of people are married to the wrong person. I'm not saying I agree with that figure, I don't know, I've never done a survey, but you would marry not just to be happy or for other life purposes as well. If your person will encourage and celebrate your wins in life and you can do the same for them, does it matter if they can't cook? Well—as long as the food is not raw, poisoned, or loaded with salmonella?

Recommend or pass this book along to someone else or get and gift the companion workbook to this volume. Both, when used together would make a great workshop or course for young daters and those who have made mistakes before and don't want to make the same boo-boos again.

END.

Relationship Books by this Author

Matters of the Heart, Made Perfect in Love
https://a.co/d/70MQW3O

Love Breaks Your Heart https://a.co/d/4KvuQLZ,
Unbreak My Heart https://a.co/d/84ceZ6M

Broken Spirits & Dry Bones https://a.co/d/e6iedNP

200 RED FLAGS: THE TRACK IS NOT SAFE How to spot red flags in relationships, especially in dating and romantic connections. https://a.co/d/ckyuqmb

Also. the **RED FLAGS** Workbook. Full size, ample room to write. Have a RED FLAG party with your friends and conquer relationship problems.

WE GET ALONG, RIGHT? *Compatibility Reality for Couples*

Companion Workbook: **WE GET ALONG, RIGHT?** *The Workbook for Couples Who Think They Do*

Relationship-related Prayerbooks by this author

While most books by this author have prayer points either throughout the book or at the end, there are some books that are only prayers. You just open up the book and pray.

Prayers Against Barrenness: *For Success in Business and Life*

Fruit of the Womb: *Prayers Against Barrenness*

Beauty Curses, *Warfare Prayers Against*
https://a.co/d/5Xlc20M

Courts of Marriage: Prayers for Marriage in the Courts of Heaven *(prayerbook)*
https://a.co/d/cNAdgAq

Courtroom Warfare @ Midnight *(prayerbook)*
https://a.co/d/5fc7Qdp

Other books by this author

Already Married in the Spirit: *Why You May Not Be Married in the Natural* https://a.co/d/gVSzfQ2

Anti-Marriage, *The Spirit of* https://a.co/d/fEKrHFu

Backstabbers https://a.co/d/gi8iBxf

Barrenness, *Prayers Against* https://a.co/d/feUltIs

Battlefield of Marriage, *The*

Blindsided: *Has the Old Man Bewitched You?* https://a.co/d/5O2fLLR

Break Free from Collective Captivity

Broken Spirits & Dry Bones

By Means of a Whorish Father https://a.co/d/hYlfR8b

Casting Down Imaginations

DANGERS OF SEX (The) https://a.co/d/d3dqoMk

Deliverance Journal

https://a.co/d/72UEUpt *Freshwater Journals*

Devil Loves Trauma, *The*

Devil Weapons: Unforgiveness, Bitterness,…

Dream Defilement

Evil Touch

Fantasy Spirit Spouse https://a.co/d/hW7oYbX

FAT Demons (The): *Breaking Demonic Curses* https://a.co/d/4kP8wV1

got LOVE? Verses for Life

Has My Soul Been Sold? https://a.co/d/dyB8hhA

Hidden Sins: Hidden Iniquity

https://a.co/d/4Mth0wa

Love Breaks Your Heart

Made Perfect In Love

Marriage Ed. Rules of Engagement & Marriage

Made Perfect in Love

Money Hunters: Beware of Those

Players Gonna Play

Second Marriage, Third--, *Any Marriage*

https://a.co/d/6m6GN4N

Seducing Spirits: Idolatry & Whoredoms

https://a.co/d/4Jq4WEs

Six Men Short: What Has Happened to all the Men?

Sleep Afflictions & Really Bad Dreams
https://a.co/d/f8sDmgv

Too Many Wives: *Why You Have Lady Problems*

Tormenting Spirits https://a.co/d/dAogEJf

Unbreak My Heart: *Don't Let Me Die*

Unseen Life, *The*

Why Do I Keep Meeting the Same Guy?

https://a.co/d/0BcAWmW

WTH? Get Me Out of This Hell

https://a.co/d/a7WBGJh

Unauthorized Use: This Could Be Why You Are Not Married Yet https://a.co/d/edro52M

Unbreak My Heart: *Don't Let Me Die*

 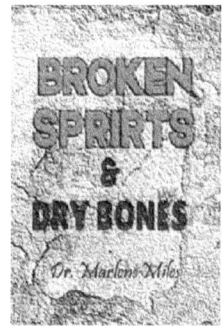 

Other Series

Spirit Spouse books

https://a.co/d/9VehDSo

https://a.co/d/97sKOwm

Battlefield of Marriage, The

https://a.co/d/eUDzizO

Players Gonna Play

https://a.co/d/2hzGw3N

<u>*Sent*</u> **Spirit Spouse** (can someone send you a spirit spouse? This book is not yet released.)

The Wilderness Romance *(series)* This series is about conducting a Godly relationship and marriage with someone who is a Wilderness person. It is about how to recognize it and navigate through it. These books are about how not to get caught up in such.

- *The Social Wilderness*
- *The Sexual Wilderness*
- *The Spiritual Wilderness*